This informational booklet provides a general overview of a particular topic related to OSHA standards. It does not alter or determine compliance responsibilities in OSHA standards or the *Occupational Safety and Health Act of 1970*. Because interpretations and enforcement policy may change over time, you should consult current OSHA administrative interpretations and decisions by the Occupational Safety and Health Review Commission and the Courts for additional guidance on OSHA compliance requirements.

This information is available to sensory impaired individuals upon request.
Voice phone: (202) 693-1999; teletypewriter (TTY) number: (877) 889-5627.

www.osha.gov

Underground Construction (Tunneling)

U.S. Department of Labor
Elaine L. Chao, Secretary

Occupational Safety and Health Administration
John L. Henshaw, Assistant Secretary

OSHA 3115-06R
2003

Contents

Introduction

The construction of underground tunnels, shafts, chambers, and passageways are essential yet dangerous activities. Working under reduced light conditions, difficult or limited access and egress, with the potential for exposure to air contaminants and the hazards of fire and explosion, underground construction workers face many dangers. To help employers protect the safety and health of underground construction workers, the Occupational Safety and Health Administration (OSHA) has prepared a number of guidance documents, including the underground construction regulations, found in Part 1926, section 800 of Title 29 of the Code of Federal Regulations (29 CFR 1926.800).

OSHA regulations relating to underground construction were originally adopted in 1971 and revised over the years to add new protective measures and enhance worker safety. This publication summarizes OSHA's regulations related to underground construction. As such, it should be used as a guide but not as a substitute for the complete text of 29 CFR 1926.800.

Construction operations covered by the OSHA standard

The OSHA underground construction regulation (29 CFR 1926.800) applies to the construction of underground tunnels, shafts, chambers, and passageways. It also applies to cut-and-cover excavations connected to ongoing underground construction as well as those that create conditions characteristic of underground construction. These hazards include reduced natural ventilation and light, difficult and limited access and egress, exposure to air contaminants, fire, flooding, and explosion. The regulation does not apply to excavation and trenching operations for above ground structures that are not physically connected to an underground construction operation or to underground electrical transmission and distribution lines.

OSHA has developed the following definitions for construction activities that fall within the underground construction field:

A tunnel is "an excavation beneath the surface of the ground, the longer axis of which makes an angle not greater than 20 degrees to the horizontal."

A shaft is "(1) a passage made from the surface of the ground to a point underground, the longer axis of which makes an angle greater than 20 degrees to the horizontal; or (2) a pit in which there are employees, and it is foreseeable that they may enter (or do enter) the horizontal excavation; or (3) a pit that has typical underground construction hazards and is connected to a horizontal excavation."

Employers and employees covered by the OSHA standard

In general, OSHA authority extends to all private sector employers with one or more employees, as well as to civilian employees in federal agencies. As such, OSHA coverage applies to employers and employees in the construction industry. Workers not covered by OSHA include the self-employed; public employees of state and local governments; employees whose working conditions are regulated by other federal agencies, such as mine workers and atomic energy workers; and immediate family members of farming operations that do not employ outside workers.

States can administer their own occupational safety and health programs through plans approved by the Department of Labor under section 18(b) of the Occupational Safety and Health (OSH) Act of 1970, but they must enforce standards that are at least as effective as federal requirements. In 2003, 26 states operated their own safety and health programs under approved programs. (See OSHA's website at www.osha.gov for a list of those states.) Of these, 23 states cover both private and public employees while three states cover only public sector employees.

State safety and health standards under approved plans must either be identical to or at least as effective as federal OSHA standards.

Requirements of the OSHA standard

The underground construction standard covers many topics of concern to those who work in the challenging environment of underground construction. A sampling of items covered by the standard includes requirements for safe access and egress routes, employee training in hazard recognition, a "check-in/check-out" procedure, and emergency procedures. This booklet summarizes all requirements of the standard.

The standard provides some flexibility in methods to control workplace hazards in underground construction as long as appropriate precautions are taken to protect workers in a variety of situations. OSHA requires that a "competent person" be responsible for carrying out several requirements of the underground construction regulations. Situations that require intervention by a "competent person" are identified in the following sections.

The need for a "competent person"

The definition of a "competent person" in 29 CFR 1926.32 (f) is as follows:

One who is capable of identifying existing and predictable hazards in the surroundings or working conditions which are unsanitary, hazardous, or dangerous to employees, and who has authorization to take prompt correctivemeasures to eliminate them.

Under Subpart S, Underground Construction, caissons, cofferdams, and compressed air, a competent person is responsible for inspecting and evaluating workplace conditions, including air monitoring and the presence of air contaminants, ground stability, and the drilling, hauling and hoisting of equipment, to identify and correct any deficiencies.

Training requirements

All employees involved in underground construction must be trained to recognize and respond to hazards associated with this type of work. Training should be tailored to the specific requirements of the jobsite and include any unique issues or requirements.

The following topics should be part of an underground construction employee training program:

- Air monitoring and ventilation
- Illumination
- Communications
- Flood control
- Personal protective equipment
- Emergency procedures, including evacuation plans
- Check-in/check-out procedures
- Explosives
- Fire prevention and protection
- Mechanical equipment

Notification and communication requirements

Any time an employer receives a notification of a hazardous condition, all oncoming shifts must be notified of occurrences or conditions that either have affected or might affect their safety. Examples of this type of situation include equipment failures, earth or rockslides, cave-ins, flooding, fires, explosions, or release of gas.

The employer must also maintain open lines of communication with other employers at the worksite to ensure a rapid and complete exchange of information concerning events or situations that may impact worker safety.

Employers must maintain lines of communication with employees during underground construction activities. To ensure effective communications are always available, communication systems must be tested upon initial entry of each shift to the underground and as often as necessary at a later time to ensure they are in working order. Powered communication systems must operate on an independent power supply and be installed so that the use of or disruption of any single communication device or signal location will not disrupt the operation of the system in any other location.

If natural unassisted voice communication is ineffective at any time, a power-assisted means must be used to ensure communication between the work face, the bottom of the shaft, and the surface. In the case of an individual employee working alone underground in a hazardous location who is out of range of natural unassisted voice communication and not able to be observed by other employees, the employer must provide an effective means of obtaining assistance in the event of an emergency.

All shafts being developed or used for personnel access or hoisting require two effective means of communication. In addition, hoist operators must have a closed-circuit voice communication system connected to each landing station, with speaker-microphones located so that the operator can communicate with individual stations while the hoist is in use. (See the section on cranes and hoists later in this booklet for more specific information.)

Site control procedures

Check-in/check-out procedures

The employer must maintain a check-in/check-out procedure to ensure that above ground personnel maintain an accurate accounting of the number of persons underground and to prevent unauthorized persons from gaining access to the site. This is especially important in the event of an emergency but is a common sense requirement at all times.

The only time this procedure is not required is when an underground construction project designed for human occupancy is completed to the point that permanent environmental controls are effective and any remaining construction activity does not have the potential to create an environmental hazard or structural failure in the construction area.

Any time an employee is working underground, at least one designated person must be on duty above ground. This person is responsible for calling for immediate assistance and keeping an accurate count of employees who remain underground in the event of an emergency.

Control of access and egress

In addition to establishing a check-in/check-out procedure, the employer must ensure safe access to and egress from all workstations at the construction site to protect employees from potential hazards, such as being struck by excavators, haulage machines, or other moving equipment.

To help control access, all unused openings, including chutes and man ways, must be tightly covered, bulk headed, barricaded, or fenced off, and posted with warning signs that read, "Keep Out" or similar language.

Ground support of portal and subsidence areas

Portal openings and access areas must be guarded by shoring, fencing, head walls, shotcreting or equivalent protection to ensure that employees and equipment have a safe means to access these areas. Subsidence areas must be similarly guarded by shoring, filling in, or placing barricades and warning signs to prevent entry. Adjacent areas must be scaled or secured to prevent loose soil, rock, or fractured materials from endangering portal, subsidence, and access areas.

Ground support of underground areas

A competent person must inspect the roof, face, and walls of the work areas at the beginning of each shift and as often as necessary to ensure ground stability. The competent person tasked with such inspection responsibilities must be protected from loose ground by location, ground support, or equivalent means. The ground conditions along all haulage ways and travel ways must also be inspected as frequently as necessary to ensure safe passage and loose ground considered to be hazardous to employees must be scaled, supported, or taken down.

A competent person must determine how often rock bolts need to be tested to ensure that they meet the necessary torque, taking into consideration ground conditions, distance from vibration sources, and the specific bolt system in use. Only torque wrenches should be used when torsion-dependent bolts are used for ground support.

Employees involved in installing ground support systems must be adequately protected from the hazards of loose ground. The bottoms of any support sets installed must have sufficient anchorage to prevent ground pressures from dislodging the support base. Lateral bracing (including collar bracing, tie rods, or spreaders) must be provided between immediately adjacent sets to increase stability.

Any dislodged or damaged ground supports that create a hazardous condition must be promptly repaired or replaced. The new supports must be installed before removing the damaged supports. Some type of support, such as a shield, must be used to maintain a safe travel way for employees working in dead-end areas ahead of any support replacement operations.

Ground support of shafts

Shafts and wells more than 5 feet in depth (1.53 m) entered by employees must be supported by steel casing, concrete pipe, timber, solid rock, or other suitable material. The full depth of the shaft must be supported except where it penetrates into solid rock that will not change as a result of exposure. Where the potential for shear exists, where the shaft passes through earth into solid rock in either direction, or where the shaft ends in solid rock, the casing or bracing must extend at least 5 feet (1.53 m) into the solid rock.

The casing or bracing must also extend 42 ($\pm$ 3) inches above ground level unless a standard railing is installed, the adjacent ground slopes away from the shaft collar, and barriers exist to prevent mobile equipment operating near the shaft from jumping over the bracing. If these conditions are met, the casing or bracing may be reduced to 12 inches above ground.

Fire prevention and control

In addition to the basic fire prevention and control guidance set forth in 29 CFR 1926 Subpart F, underground construction operations are subject to several specific requirements.

Open flames and fires are prohibited in underground construction areas except as permitted for welding, cutting, or other hot work operations. Smoking is prohibited unless an area is free of fire and

explosion hazards. Signage prohibiting smoking and open flames should be placed throughout work areas. Fire extinguishers of at least 4A:40B:C rating or equivalent extinguishing means must be available at the head and tail pulleys of underground belt conveyers.

All underground structures and those within 100 feet (30.48 m) of an opening to the underground must be constructed of materials with a fire resistance rating of at least one hour. Also, no flammable or combustible material may be stored above ground within 100 feet (30.48 m) of any access point to an underground operation. If space limitations make this unfeasible, the material must be positioned as far as possible from the entrance with a fire-resistant barrier that has at least a one-hour rating between the material and the opening. Alternative precautionary measures may be adopted from industry practices used under similar working conditions or measures recommended under industry consensus standards. A site hazard analysis may be helpful to determine the effectiveness of precautionary measures. Any spill of flammable or combustible material must be cleaned up immediately.

Gasoline may not be underground at any time for any purpose due to its volatile qualities. Internal combustion engines (except diesel-powered engines on mobile equipment) are prohibited underground. Acetylene, liquefied petroleum gas, and methyl acetylene propadiene stabilized gas may be used underground for welding, cutting, and other hot work if all requirements of OSHA regulations pertaining to such activities are met. (See 29 CFR 1926 Subpart J and 29 CFR 1926.800(j)(k)(m)(n) for a complete explana-tion of these requirements.) Only enough fuel gas and oxygen cylinders for welding, cutting, or hot work during a 24-hour period are allowed underground. Noncombustible barriers must be installed below such activities if they are performed in or over a shaft or rise.

Oil, grease, and diesel fuel stored underground must be kept in tightly sealed containers in fire-resistant areas at least 300 feet (91.44 m) from underground explosive magazines, and at least 100 feet (30.48 m) from shaft stations and steeply inclined passage-ways. Storage areas must be positioned or diked to ensure that if a

container breaks open, any fluids will not flow out of the storage area. Any hydraulically-actuated underground machinery must use fire-resistant hydraulic fluids unless it is protected by a fire suppression system or multi-purpose fire extinguisher rated at least 4A:40B:C and of sufficient capacity for the type and size of equipment involved.

Several specific requirements apply to the use of diesel fuel in underground construction operations, as follows:

- A surface level tank holding diesel fuel to be pumped to an underground storage site must have a maximum capacity no greater than the amount of fuel required to supply underground equipment for 24 hours.

- A surface level tank must be connected to the underground fueling station by an acceptable pipe or hose system controlled at the surface by a valve and at the bottom by a hose nozzle.

- The transfer pipe must remain empty at all times except when transferring diesel fuel.

- All hoisting operations in the shaft must be suspended during refueling operations if the supply piping in the shaft is not protected from potential damage.

Ventilation requirements

Fresh air must be supplied to all underground work areas in sufficient amounts to prevent any dangerous or harmful accumulation of dusts, fumes, mists, vapors, or gases. If natural ventilation does not provide the necessary air quality through sufficient air volume and air flow, the employer must provide mechanical ventilation to ensure that each employee working underground has at least 200 cubic feet (5.7m3) of fresh air per minute.

When performing work that is likely to produce dust, fumes, mists, vapors, or gases (such as blasting or rock drilling), the linear velocity of air flow in the tunnel bore, shafts, and all other underground work areas must be at least 30 feet (9.15 m) per minute. When such operations are complete, the ventilation systems must exhaust smoke and fumes to the outside atmosphere before

resuming work in all affected areas. When drilling rock or concrete, dust control measures such as wet drilling, vacuum collectors, and water mix spray systems must be used to maintain dust levels within limits set in 29 CFR 1926.55, which includes gases, vapors, fumes, dusts, and mists.

The direction of mechanical airflow must be reversible but ventilation doors must be designed and installed to remain closed when in use, regardless of the direction of the airflow. If the ventilation system has been shut down and all employees are removed from the underground area, only competent persons authorized to test for air contaminants may be allowed underground until the ventilation system has been restored and all affected areas have tested at acceptable limits for air contaminants.

Illumination requirements

As in all construction operations, OSHA requires that proper illumination be provided during tunneling operations (see 29 CFR 1926.56 for details). When explosives are handled, only acceptable portable lighting equipment may be used within 50 feet of any underground heading.

For general tunneling operations, a minimum illumination intensity of 5 foot-candles must be maintained, although 10 foot-candles must be provided for shaft heading during drilling, mucking, and scaling.

Special air monitoring requirements

The employer must assign a "competent person" to perform air monitoring. If this individual determines that air contaminants may present a danger to life at any time, the employer must immediately take all necessary precautions and post a notice at all entrances to the underground site about the hazardous condition.

In performing air monitoring duties, the competent person must take into consideration the location of the jobsite (its proximity to fuel tanks, sewers, gas lines, etc.); the geology of the site, including soil type and permeability; the history of the site and the construc-

tion operation (changes in levels of substances monitored over time); and work practices at the jobsite (use of diesel engines, explosives, and fuel gas; hot work, welding, and cutting; and the physical reactions of employees to working underground.

Test for oxygen first

The competent person charged with air monitoring must test for oxygen content before testing for air contaminants. All underground work areas must be tested as often as necessary to verify that the atmosphere at normal atmospheric pressure remains within the acceptable parameters of 19.5 and 22 percent oxygen.

After verifying oxygen levels, the competent person must test all underground work areas for carbon monoxide, nitrogen dioxide, hydrogen sulfide, and other toxic gases, dusts, vapors, mists, and fumes as often as necessary to ensure that levels remain within permissible exposure limits (see 29 CFR 1926.55 for detailed information on these limits).

Testing for methane and other flammable gases

The competent person must also test all underground work areas for methane and other flammable gases to determine whether the operation must be classified as potentially gassy or gassy. If the atmosphere meets the criteria for these designations, the precautions listed in the section discussing gassy or potentially gassy operations later in this booklet must be followed. Other precautions to take when testing for methane or other flammable gases include:

- If 20 percent or more of the lower explosive limit for methane or other flammable gases is detected in any underground work area or in the air return, all employees must be evacuated to a safe location above ground (except those employees required to eliminate the hazard). Electrical power (except for acceptable pumping and ventilation equipment) must be cut off to the area until concentrations reach less than 20 percent of the lower explosive limit.

- If 10 percent or more of the lower explosive limit for methane gas or other flammable gases is detected near any welding,

cutting, or other hot work, the work must be suspended until the concentration is reduced to below 10 percent of the lower explosive limit.

- When 5 percent or more of the lower explosive limit for methane or other flammable gases is detected in an underground work area or in the air return, steps should be taken to increase ventilation air volume or otherwise control the gas concentration (unless all requirements of operating under potentially gassy or gassy operations are met).

Hydrogen sulfide levels

When air monitoring reveals the presence of 5 ppm or more of hydrogen sulfide, the affected underground areas must be tested at the beginning and midpoint of each shift until the concentration is measured at less than 5 ppm for three consecutive days.

Employees must be notified if hydrogen sulfide is detected in amounts exceeding 10 ppm and a continuous sampling and indicating monitor must be used to keep track of levels. If the concentration of hydrogen sulfide reaches 20 ppm, the monitor must be designed to provide both visual and audible alarms to warn that additional measures (respirator use, increased ventilation, evacuation) may be appropriate.

Special conditions for drilling and blasting underground

Before initiating any drilling operation underground, a "competent person" must inspect all drilling and associated equipment as well as the drilling area and correct any hazards. Employees are not allowed on a drill mast when a drill bit is in operation or a drill machine is being moved. Also, when moving a drill machine, all associated equipment and tools must be secured and the mast placed in a safe position.

Working on or around jumbo decks involves special safety precautions, including the following:

- Locate all receptacles or racks to store drill steel on jumbos.

- Warn employees working below jumbo decks when drilling is about to begin.

- The top deck of a jumbo must have a mechanical way to lift unwieldy or heavy items.

- Only employees assisting the operator may ride on the jumbo unless it is equipped with seating for each passenger and protection from crushing or catching hazards.

- Jumbo decks more than 10 feet high must be equipped with guardrails on all open sides unless an adjacent surface provides fall protection. Jumbo decks and stair treads must be slip-resistant, secured, and maintained to prevent slip, trip, and fall hazards.

- Jumbos must be chocked so they will not move when employees are working on them.

Whenever an underground blasting operation in a shaft is complete, a "competent person" must check the air quality and make sure that no walls, ladders, timbers, blocking, and wedges have been loosened as a result of the activity. If repairs are required, only employees involved in repair activity may be in or below affected areas until repairs are complete.

All blasting wires must be kept clear of electrical lines, pipes, rails and other conductive material (except earth), to prevent explosions or exposure of employees to electric current.

Special requirements for using cranes and hoists underground

The OSHA standard has provisions for the use of cranes or hoists that are unique to underground construction. In addition to provisions that apply to all construction activities using cranes or hoists (29 CFR 1926.550 and 29 CFR 1926.552), cranes used in underground construction must be equipped with a limit switch to prevent overtravel at the top and bottom of the hoist way. The limit switch should only be used when operational controls malfunction. Hoist controls must be arranged so the operator can reach all

controls and the emergency power cutoff without reaching beyond his/her normal operating position.

Underground hoists must be designed to allow powering of the hoist drum in both directions and so that brakes are automatically applied upon power release or failure. The hoist operator must have a closed-circuit voice communication system with speaker microphones to communicate with individual landing stations. Also, hoists must be equipped with landing level indicators (marking the hoist rope is not adequate) and fire extinguishers (rated at least 2A:10B:C) in each hoist house.

Before using a hoist that has been out of operation for a complete shift or after repair or service, the operator must test run the equipment and correct any unsafe conditions before use. Inspections and load testing to 100 percent of capacity must be performed at least annually and after any repairs or alterations affecting the structural integrity of the hoist.

For material hoists, wire rope used in load lines must support at least five times the maximum intended load or the factor recommended by the rope manufacturer, whichever is greater. Personnel hoists must have at least two means to stop the load, each able to stop and hold 150 percent of the hoists' rated line pull. For personnel hoisting, a broken-rope safety, safety catch, or arrestment device are not adequate means of stopping.

Other aspects of hoist safety that apply to underground construction include:

- Employees may not ride on top of any cage, skip, or bucket unless inspecting or maintaining the system and wearing a safety belt or harness.

- Personnel and materials must be hoisted separately (except small tools and supplies secured in a nonhazardous manner).

- When sinking shafts 75 feet (22.86 m) or less, cages, skips, and buckets that may swing, bump, or snag against shaft sides must be guided by fenders, rails, ropes, or a combination. If the shaft is more than 75 feet, hoisted objects must be rope- or rail-guided for the full length of travel.

Additional safety requirements for personnel hoists in under-ground operations include:

■ The operator must be able to see and hear signals at the operator's station.

■ All cages must be equipped with a steel-plate protective canopy that slopes to the outside and can be pushed up for emergency egress and have a locking door that opens only inward.

■ The sides of personnel cages must be enclosed by 1/2 inch wire mesh to a height of at least 6 feet (1.83 m). If the cage is being used as a work platform and is not in motion, the sides may be reduced to 42 inches (1.07 m).

■ During sinking operations in shafts where guides and safeties are not used, the personnel platform may not exceed 200 feet (60.96 m) per minute and governors must be used during personnel hoisting. The speed may increase to 600 feet (182.88 m) per minute when guides and safeties are used and greater speeds when shafts are complete.

Potential hazards that require special precautions

Gassy or potentially gassy operations

Gassy or potentially gassy operations present specific hazards to underground construction workers. It is essential that employers understand the terms "gassy" and "potentially gassy" and to know what precautions to take when dealing with such environments. Operations that meet the criteria for this hazardous classification must be equipped with ventilation systems constructed with fire-resistant materials; have acceptable electrical systems, including fan motors; and have above ground controls to reverse the air flow. When using a mine-type ventilation system with an offset main fan on the surface, the system must be equipped with explosion doors or a weak-wall with an area at least equivalent to the cross-sectional area of the airway.

Gassy operations occur under the following conditions:

- When air monitoring discloses 10 percent or more of the lower explosive limit for methane or other flammable gases measured at 12 inches (304.8 mm) ± 0.25 inch (6.35 mm) from the roof, face, floor, or walls in any underground work area for three consecutive days; or

- There has been an ignition of methane or other flammable gases emanating from the strata that indicates the presence of such gases; or

- The underground construction operation is connected to an underground work area classified as gassy and subject to a continuous course of air that contains the flammable gas concentration.

The underground construction standard requires that gassy operations meet several special requirements, including both personnel and equipment safety concerns. These requirements include:

- Entrances to a gassy operation must be marked with prominently posted signage that identifies the area as gassy.

- Maintain a fire watch when performing hot work (welding, cutting, heating) in a gassy area and for a sufficient period after completing the work to ensure no possibility of fire remains. (See 29 CFR 1926.352(e))

- Use only acceptable equipment in well-maintained condition. Any mobile diesel-powered equipment must either be approved by MSHA and meet the requirements of 30 CFR part 36 (formerly Schedule 31) or the employer must demonstrate that the equipment is fully equivalent to MSHA-approved equipment and operated according to these regulations.

- Smoking is prohibited in all gassy operations; the employer must collect all possible sources of ignition (matches, lighters, etc.) from any person entering a gassy operation area.

- All operations in the affected area must stop when an operation is classified as gassy until full compliance with gassy operation requirements is confirmed or the operation is downgraded to a potentially gassy operation (see the following section). The only

exceptions are operations to control the gas concentration, installation of above ground equipment to reverse the airflow, or actions to comply with gassy operation requirements.

Gassy operations can be downgraded to potentially gassy when air monitoring results remain below 10 percent of the lower explosive limit for methane or other flammable gases for three consecutive days.

Potentially gassy operations, such as an unexpected pocket of gas, occur when the following conditions exist:

- Air monitoring shows 10 percent or more of the lower explosive limit for methane or other flammable gases measured at 12 inches (304.8 mm) ± 0.25 inch (6.35 mm) from the roof, face, floor or walls in any underground work area for more than a 24-hour period.

- The history of the geographical area, geological formation, or past experience indicates that 10 percent or more of the lower explosive limit for methane or other flammable gases is likely to be encountered in such underground operations.

Both gassy and potentially gassy operations require special air monitoring actions under the guidance of a "competent person," including testing for oxygen and flammable gas content in the affected underground work areas and adjacent work areas at the beginning and midpoint of each work shift. A manual flammable gas monitor should be used for gas testing and a manual electrical shut down control must be provided near the heading for the gas monitor.

The use of rapid excavation machines requires continuous automatic flammable gas monitoring to monitor the air at the heading, on the rib, and in the return air duct. If 20 percent or more of the lower explosive limit for methane or other flammable gases is encountered, the continuous monitor alert should signal the heading and shut down electrical power in the affected underground work area (except for required pumping and ventilation equipment).

Local gas tests must be conducted before and throughout welding, cutting or other hot work. In underground operations

driven by drill-and-blast methods, the air in the affected area must be continuously tested for flammable gas when employees are working in the area as well as before reentering after blasting operations.

Emergency procedures

Whenever an employee is working underground at least one designated person must be on duty above ground, responsible for maintaining an accurate count of the number of employees underground and summoning emergency aid if needed. Every employee working underground must have a portable hand lamp or cap lamp for emergency use unless natural light or an emergency lighting system provides adequate illumination for escape. Employers must provide self-rescuers approved by the National Institute for Occupational Safety and Health (NIOSH) in all underground work areas where employees might be trapped by smoke or gas. (See CFR 1926.103 for more information.)

If 25 or more employees work underground at one time, the employer must provide at least two 5-person rescue teams, one at the jobsite or within 30 minutes travel time from the entry point to the site and the other team within two hours travel time. If less than 25 employees work underground, the employer must have one 5-person rescue team at the jobsite or within 30 minutes travel time. In both situations, advance arrangements can be made for local rescue services to meet this requirement. Rescue team members must be trained in rescue procedures, the use and limitations of breathing apparatus, and the use of firefighting equipment with qualifications reviewed annually. When flammable or noxious gases are anticipated at a jobsite, rescue teams must practice using self-contained breathing apparatus once a month. The rescue teams must be available through the duration of a construction project.

If a shaft is used as the means of egress, the employer must arrange for a readily available power-assisted hoisting capability in case of emergency, unless the regular hoisting means will function in the event of a power failure.

Recordkeeping requirements

Records of all air quality tests must be maintained above ground at the worksite and be available on request to the Secretary of Labor or his or her representative. The record must include the location, date, time, substance and amount monitored. Records of exposures to toxic substances must be kept for 30 years. (See 29 CFR 1910.1020 for more detailed information on access to employee exposure and medical records.) All other air quality test records must be retained until the project is complete.

Inspection certification records for all hoist equipment indicating the date of the most recent inspection and load-test, the signature of the person performing the inspection and test, and a serial number or other identifier for the hoist must be maintained on file until the project is complete.

OSHA assistance

OSHA can provide extensive help through a variety of programs, including technical assistance about effective safety and health programs, state plans, workplace consultations, voluntary protection programs, strategic partnerships, and training and education, and more. An overall commitment to workplace safety and health can add value to your business, to your workplace, and to your life.

Safety and health management system guidelines

Effective management of worker safety and health protection is a decisive factor in reducing the extent and severity of work-related injuries and illnesses and their related costs. To assist employers and employees in developing effective safety and health programs, OSHA published recommended Safety and Health Program Management Guidelines (Federal Register 54 (16): 3904-3916, January 26, 1989). These voluntary guidelines can be applied to all places of employment covered by OSHA.

The guidelines identify four general elements critical to the development of a successful safety and health management system:

- Management leadership and employee involvement.
- Worksite analysis.
- Hazard prevention and control.
- Safety and health training.

The guidelines recommend specific actions, under each of these general elements, to achieve an effective safety and health program. The Federal Register notice is available online at www.osha.gov.

State programs

The Occupational Safety and Health Act of 1970 (OSH Act) encourages states to develop and operate their own job safety and health plans. OSHA approves and monitors these plans. There are currently 26 state plans: 23 cover both private and public (state and local government) employment; 3 states, Connecticut, New Jersey, and New York, cover the public sector only. States and territories with their own OSHA-approved occupational safety and health plans must adopt standards identical to, or at least as effective as, the federal standards.

OSHA consultation services

Consultation assistance is available on request to employers who want help in establishing and maintaining a safe and healthful workplace. Largely funded by OSHA, the service is provided at no cost to the employer. Primarily developed for smaller employers with more hazardous operations, the consultation service is delivered by state governments employing professional safety and health consultants. Comprehensive assistance includes an appraisal of all-mechanical systems, work practices, and occupational safety and health hazards of the workplace and all aspects of the employer's present job safety and health program. In addition, the service offers assistance to employers in developing and imple-

menting an effective safety and health program. No penalties are proposed or citations issued for hazards identified by the consultant. OSHA provides consultation assistance to the employer with the assurance that his or her name and firm and any information about the workplace will not be routinely reported to OSHA enforcement staff.

Under the consultation program, certain exemplary employers may request participation in OSHA's Safety and Health Achievement Recognition Program (SHARP). Eligibility for participation in SHARP includes receiving a comprehensive consultation visit, demonstrating exemplary achievements in workplace safety and health by abating all identified hazards, and developing an excellent safety and health program.

Employers accepted into SHARP may receive an exemption from programmed inspections (not complaint or accident investigation inspections) for one year. For more information concerning consultation assistance, call 800-321-OSHA or visit www.osha.gov.

The OSHA Voluntary Protection Program (VPP)

Voluntary Protection Programs and onsite consultation services, when coupled with an effective enforcement program, expand worker protection to help meet the goals of the OSH Act. The three levels of VPP, Star, Merit, and Demonstration, are designed to recognize outstanding achievements by companies that have successfully incorporated comprehensive safety and health programs into their total management system. The VPP motivates others to achieve excellent safety and health results and establish a cooperative relationship between employers, employees, and OSHA.

For additional information on VPP and how to apply, contact the OSHA regional offices listed at the end of this publication or call 800-321-OSHA or visit www.osha.gov.

Strategic Partnership Programs

OSHA's Strategic Partnership Program, the newest member of OSHA's cooperative programs, helps encourage, assist, and recognize the efforts of partners to eliminate serious workplace hazards and achieve a high level of worker safety and health. Whereas OSHA's Consultation Program and VPP entail one-on-one relationships between OSHA and individual work sites, most strategic partnerships seek to have a broader impact by building cooperative relationships with groups of employers and employees. These partnerships are voluntary, cooperative relationships between OSHA, employers, employee representatives, and others (e.g., trade unions, trade and professional associations, universities, and other government agencies).

For more information on this and other cooperative programs, contact your nearest OSHA office, call 800-321-OSHA, or visit www.osha.gov.

The OSHA Alliance Program

Alliances enable organizations committed to workplace safety and health to collaborate with OSHA to prevent injuries and illnesses in the workplace. OSHA and its allies work together to reach out to, educate, and lead the nation's employers and their employees in improving and advancing workplace safety and health.

Alliances are open to all, including trade or professional organiza- tions, businesses, labor organizations, educational institutions, and government agencies. In some cases, organizations may be building on existing relationships with OSHA through other cooper- ative programs.

There are few formal program requirements for alliances, which are less structured than other cooperative agreements, and the agreements do not include an enforcement component. However, OSHA and the participating organizations must define, implement, and meet a set of short- and long-term goals that fall into three cat- egories: training and education; outreach and communication; and promotion of the national dialogue on workplace safety and health.

OSHA training and education

OSHA area offices offer a variety of information services, such as compliance assistance, technical advice, publications, audiovisual aids and speakers for special engagements. OSHA's Training Institute in Des Plaines, IL, provides basic and advanced courses in safety and health for federal and state compliance officers, state consultants, federal agency personnel, and private sector employers, employees, and their representatives.

The OSHA Training Institute also has established OSHA Training Institute Education Centers to address the increased demand for its courses from the private sector and from other federal agencies. These centers are nonprofit colleges, universities, and other organizations that have been selected after a competition for participation in the program.

OSHA also provides funds to nonprofit organizations, through grants, to conduct workplace training and education in subjects where OSHA believes there is a lack of workplace training. Grants are awarded annually. Grant recipients are expected to contribute 20 percent of the total grant cost.

For more information on grants, training, and education, contact the OSHA Training Institute, Office of Training and Education, 1555 Times Drive, Des Plaines, IL 60018, (847) 297-4810. For further information on any OSHA program, contact your nearest OSHA office.

Information available electronically

OSHA has a variety of materials and tools available on its website at www.osha.gov. These include e-Tools such as Expert Advisors, Electronic Compliance Assistance Tools (e-cats), Technical Links; regulations, directives, publications; videos, and other information for employers and employees. OSHA's software programs and compliance assistance tools walk you through challenging safety and health issues and common problems to find the best solutions for your workplace.

OSHA publications

OSHA has an extensive publications program. For a listing of free or sales items, visit OSHA's website at www.osha.gov or contact the OSHA Publications Office, U.S. Department of Labor, 200 Constitution Avenue NW, N-3101, Washington, DC 20210. Telephone (202) 693-1888 or fax to (202) 693-2498.

Contacting OSHA

To report an emergency, file a complaint, or seek OSHA advice, assistance, or products, call (800) 321-OSHA or contact the nearest OSHA regional or area office listed at the end of this publication. The teletypewriter (TTY) number is (877) 889-5627.

You can also file a complaint online and obtain more information on OSHA federal and state programs by visiting OSHA's website at www.osha.gov.

For more information on grants, training, and education, contact the OSHA Training Institute, Office of Training and Education, 1555 Times Drive, Des Plaines, IL 60018, (847) 297-4810, or see Outreach on OSHA's website at www.osha.gov.

OSHA Regional Offices

Region I
(CT,* ME, MA, NH, RI, VT*)
Boston, MA 02203
(617) 565-9860

Region II
(NJ,* NY,* PR,* VI*)
201 Varick Street, Room 670
New York, NY 10014
(212) 337-2378

Region III
(DE, DC, MD,* PA,* VA,* WV)
The Curtis Center
170 S. Independence Mall West
Suite 740 West
Philadelphia, PA 19106-3309
(215) 861-4900

Region IV
(AL, FL, GA, KY,* MS, NC,* SC,* TN*)
Atlanta Federal Center
61 Forsyth Street SW, Room 6T50
Atlanta, GA 30303
(404) 562-2300

Region V
(IL, IN,* MI,* MN,* OH, WI)
230 South Dearborn Street, Room 3244
Chicago, IL 60604
(312) 353-2220

Region VI
(AR, LA, NM,* OK, TX)
525 Griffin Street, Room 602
Dallas, TX 75202
(214) 767-4731 or 4736 x224

Region VII
(IA,* KS, MO, NE)
City Center Square
1100 Main Street, Suite 800
Kansas City, MO 64105
(816) 426-5861

Region VIII
(CO, MT, ND, SD, UT,* WY*)
1999 Broadway, Suite 1690
PO Box 46550
Denver, CO 80202-5716
(303) 844-1600

Region IX
(American Samoa, AZ,* CA,* HI, NV,* Northern Mariana Islands)
71 Stevenson Street, Room 420
San Francisco, CA 94105
(415) 975-4310

Region X
(AK,* ID, OR,* WA*)
1111 Third Avenue, Suite 715
Seattle, WA 98101-3212
(206) 553-5930

*These states and territories operate their own OSHA-approved job safety and health programs (Connecticut, New Jersey, and New York plans cover public employees only). States with approved programs must have a standard that is identical to, or at least as effective as, the federal standard.

Note: To get contact information for OSHA Area Offices, OSHA-approved state plans, and OSHA Consultation Projects, please visit us online at www.osha.gov or call us at (800) 321-OSHA.

www.ingramcontent.com/pod-product-compliance
Lightning Source LLC
Chambersburg PA
CBHW051828170526
45167CB00005B/2200